FASCINATING SCIENCE PROJECTS

SOUND

Bobbi Searle

Franklin Watts
London • Sydney

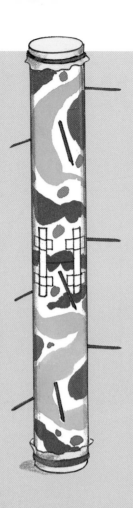

© Aladdin Books Ltd 2002
Produced by
Aladdin Books Ltd
28 Percy Street
London W1T 2BZ

ISBN 0–7496–4494–X

First published in Great Britain in 2002 by
Franklin Watts
96 Leonard Street
London
EC2A 4XD

Designers:
Flick, Book Design and Graphics
Ian Thompson

Editor:
Harriet Brown

Illustrators:
Catherine Ward
and Peter Wilks – SGA
Cartoons:
Tony Kenyon – BL Kearley

Consultant:
Bryson Gore

Printed in UAE

A CIP catalogue record for this book is available
from the British Library.

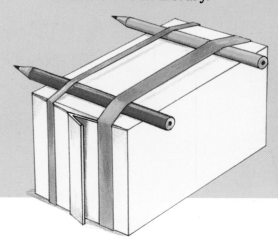

Contents

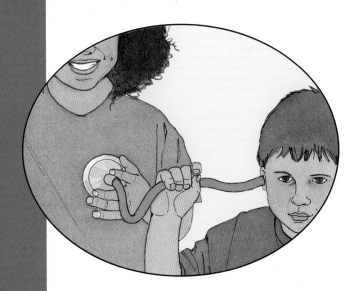

Introduction

In this book, the science of sound is explained through a series of fascinating projects and experiments. Each chapter deals with a different topic on sound and contains a major project that is supported by simple experiments, 'Magic panels' and 'Fascinating fact boxes'. At the end of every chapter there is an explanation of what has happened and what this means. Projects requiring sharp tools should be done under adult supervision.

This states the purpose of the project

METHOD NOTES
Helpful hints on things to remember when carrying out your project.

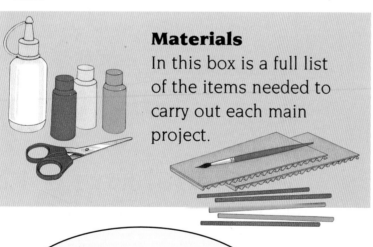

Materials
In this box is a full list of the items needed to carry out each main project.

1. The steps that describe how to carry out each project are listed clearly as numbered points.
2. Where there are illustrations to help you understand the instructions, the text refers to them as 'Figure 1', etc.

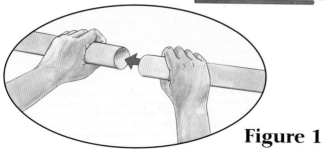

Figure 1

Figure 2

THE AMAZING MAGIC PANEL
This heading states what is happening

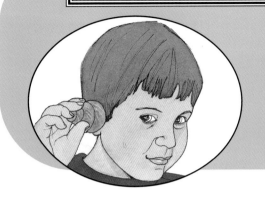

These boxes contain an activity or experiment that has a particularly dramatic or surprising result!

WHY IT WORKS
You can find out exactly what happened here too.

WHY IT WORKS

These boxes explain what happened during your project, and explain the meaning of the result.

Fascinating facts!
An amusing or surprising fact related to the theme of the chapter.

Where the project involves using a sharp object or anything else that requires adult supervision, you will see this warning symbol.

The text in these circles links the theme of the topic from one page to the next in the chapter.

What is sound?

From the quietest mouse to the noisiest rocket, sound is all around us. Even if you went to the quietest place in the world you could never escape it. Sound is a form of energy. It is caused when something is made to move backwards and forwards. This movement is called vibration. The air around the object vibrates and the vibrating air carries the sound to your ear.

Make panpipes to discover one way of creating sound

METHOD NOTES
Take time to cut the straws carefully so that they vary in length gradually.

Materials
- straws
- scissors
- glue
- paints
- a paintbrush
- 2 pieces of corrugated card cut into the shapes shown

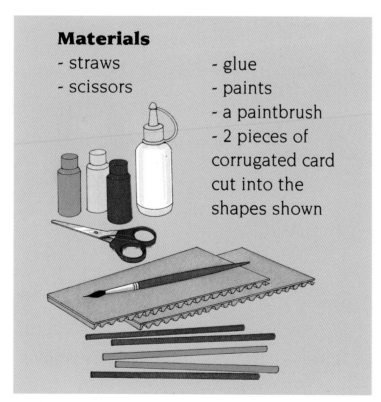

1. Take five straws. Leave one the length it is. Cut a piece from the next one so that it is slightly shorter than the first straw (Figure 1).

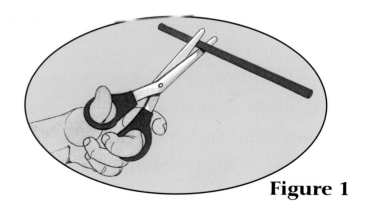

Figure 1

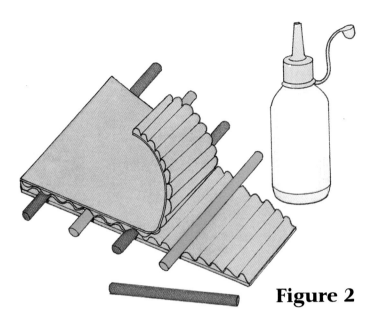

Figure 2

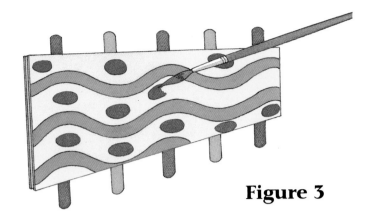

Figure 3

2. Do the same with each straw so that you end up with five straws that gradually get shorter.

3. Glue the straws onto one piece of card in order of length (Figure 2).

4. Glue the second piece of card on top of the straws (Figure 2).

5. Use paints to decorate the card with a design or pattern (Figure 3).

6. Blow across the top of the straws (Figure 4).

WHY IT WORKS

As you blow across the straws tops, the air inside them vibrates. Each straw makes a different sound. This is because air in the short straws vibrates faster than air in the long straws. The faster something vibrates, the higher the sound. So shorter straws create higher sounds and longer straws create lower sounds.

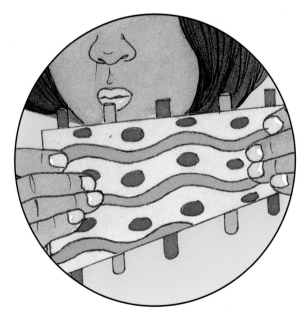

Figure 4

7. Listen to how the different lengths of straw make different sounds.

What is sound?

You can make sound in lots of different ways. You can shout, clap your hands or whistle. All these different noises are types of sound waves caused by vibration.

SOUND WAVE DETECTOR

Carefully remove both ends of an empty tin can. Cut a circle from a balloon and stretch it over one end. Secure it in place with an elastic band (Figure 1).

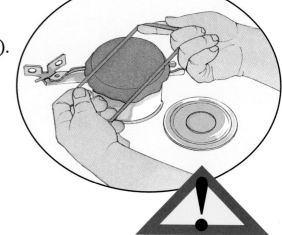

Figure 1

Glue a small mirror to the centre of the balloon (Figure 2). Place the tin on a hard surface.

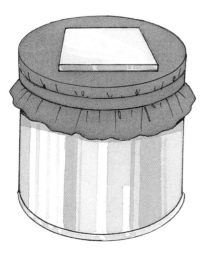

Figure 2

WHY IT WORKS

When you shout near the tin, you make air vibrate and create sound waves. These waves travel through the air to the tin. They make the balloon surface vibrate, causing the mirror to shake and move the light reflected on the wall.

Turn off the lights and shine a torch at the mirror. Angle the torch so that the light reflects onto a wall (Figure 3). Ask someone to shout near the tin. Watch how the reflection on the wall moves.

Figure 3

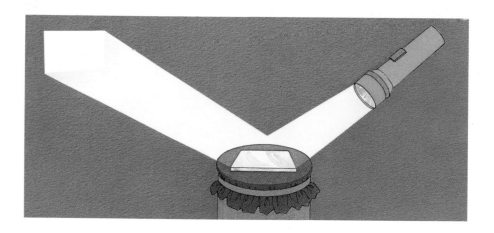

SOUND THROUGH A SPOON

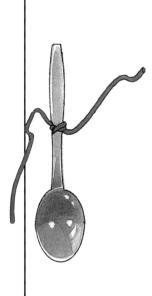

Tie a piece of string to a spoon. Wrap the ends of the string around your index fingers. Place your index fingers in your ears. Tap the spoon against a table. Listen carefully. The vibrations from the spoon travel through the string straight into your ears so the sound you hear is loud.

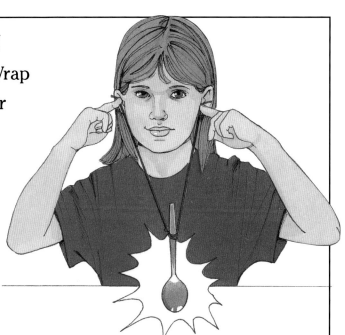

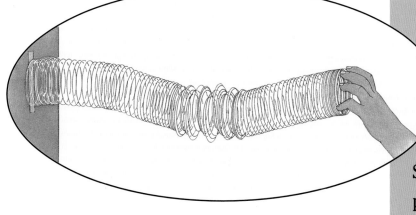

RECREATE SOUND WAVES

Tape one end of a Slinky to a wall. Hold the other end and stretch the Slinky.

Give the Slinky a push and then a pull. Watch what happens to the Slinky as it is compressed and stretched.

WHY IT WORKS

You will see a pulse move along the Slinky to the far end at the wall and then bounces back. If you send a slow pulse down the Slinky you will see an irregular pattern of pulses. If you speed the pulse up you will see waves appear along the Slinky at different intervals. Sound waves travel in this way. When you hit an object, it vibrates and pushes and pulls the air around it. Each layer of air bumps into the next layer. This makes different layers of air pressure – sound waves. These waves carry the sound to your ears.

See how sound travels

MAKING WAVES

Find a large, flat, smooth surface. Arrange four marbles in a line. Make sure they are all touching each other. Flick a fifth marble towards one end of the line of marbles (Figure 1).

Figure 1

Make sure you flick it hard enough so that it hits the end marble (Figure 1).

Watch what happens to the marble at the other end of the line (Figure 2).

Figure 2

WHY IT WORKS

The marble you flick is carrying energy. When it hits the end of the row of marbles, it passes its energy on. This energy is transferred through the row.

When it gets to the last marble, this marble moves off. This is how sound is carried through air. When air vibrates, energy is passed from one air molecule to the next until the energy has run out.

I can hear you!

Did you know that you can hear horses approaching long before they arrive by putting your ear to the ground and listening?

THE AMAZING JUMPING SALT
See how sound waves can travel

Take the tin with the balloon stretched over it on page 8. Sprinkle some salt on the balloon. Hold another can close to the salt and tap the side of it with a ruler. Watch as the salt moves all by itself.

WHY IT WORKS

The sound waves you create make the balloon vibrate. The salt is light and will jump as the surface of the balloon vibrates.

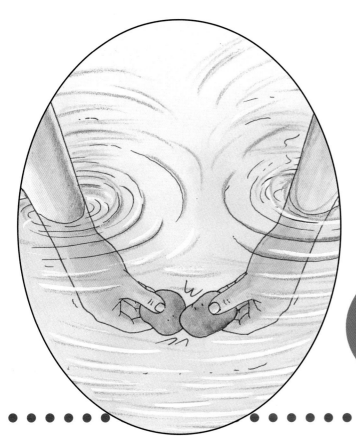

SOUND WAVES IN WATER

Find two stones. Run a bath, sit in it and bang the stones together under water. Listen to the sound. Now lie down in the bath with your ears under water. Bang the stones together under water. Is the sound louder when you hear it through water?

Sound travels in waves. It travels better through solids and liquids than it does through air. So, sounds seem louder when you hear them through solids or liquids.

Speed of sound

Sound travels through the air at around 350 metres per second. When you go to a cricket match or an air show, you see the player hit the ball and see the aeroplanes before the sound reaches your ears. It takes nearly 3 seconds for sound to travel a kilometre. We are able to hear echoes (see pages 34-37) only because sound travels so slowly.

Follow this project to work out the speed of sound

METHOD NOTES
You will need a partner to help in doing the calculations.

Materials
- two pieces of wood
- two strips of card
- sticky tape
- tape measure
- stopwatch
- notepad
- pencil

1. Place the pieces of wood on a table.
2. Tape a strip of card to the middle of each piece of wood as shown (Figure 1) to make a handle.
3. Find a building with a large, flat outside wall.

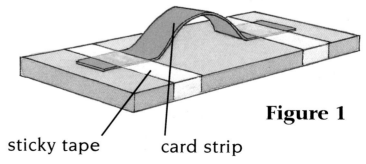

sticky tape   card strip

Figure 1

Figure 2

4. Stand facing the wall and clap the two pieces of wood together (Figure 2). Try standing at different distances from the wall until you get a good echo – you may need to be around 20-30 m away.

Figure 3

5. Using the tape measure, ask a friend to measure and record how far from the wall you are standing.

6. Clap the pieces of wood together and listen for the noise as the sound is reflected back from the wall towards you.

7. When you hear the reflected sound, clap again. Synchronise your claps with the echo you hear.

Figure 4

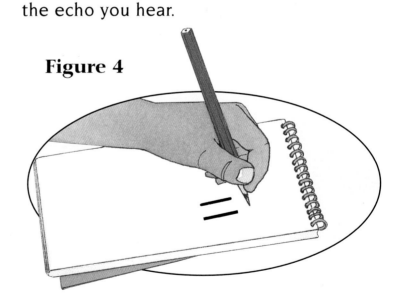

8. Still synchronising your claps, ask your friend to time (Figure 3) and record (Figure 4) how long it takes to do 10 claps.

WHAT THIS SHOWS

To find the speed of sound: (a) Find the distance to and from the wall by multiplying the distance between you and the wall by 2. (b) Find the time it took for the sound to travel once to and from the wall by dividing the time you measured by 10. (c) Calculate the speed of sound by dividing the distance you found in (a) by the time you found in (b). It should be about 350 metres/sec.

Speed of sound

The speed of fast fighter planes is measured using the speed of sound. If they can fly at the speed of sound they are travelling at Mach 1.

DOPPLER EFFECT

Ask your friend to cycle past you slowly blowing a whistle. Listen to the sound as he or she goes past. Now ask your friend to cycle past you quickly. Make sure they are still blowing the whistle. How does the sound change as they come towards and go away from you?

What's that bang?
The first person to fly faster than the speed of sound was Chuck Yeager in 1947. His plane made a huge sonic boom and people thought his plane had crashed.

WHY IT WORKS

More vibrations reach you each second when the whistle is getting nearer, making the sound higher. As it moves away, fewer vibrations reach you each second, making the sound lower. This is the Doppler effect.

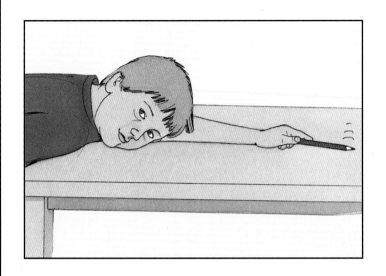

SPEED OF SOUND EXPERIMENTS

Stand at one end of a table. Lean over and tap a pencil on the table. Now lean over and put your ear on the table. Tap the pencil on the table. Is the sound louder when you hear it through the table? Sound waves travel many times faster in solids than they do in air.

BOUNCING SOUND EXPERIMENT

Stand at arm's length from a wall with your right side facing it. Put the end of a card tube to your left ear and close your eyes. Ask your partner to tap two rulers together on the left side near the end of the tube. Then put the tube to your right ear so that it is pointing at the wall. Ask them to tap the rulers about 30 cm from your left ear. How does this sound different to the first time?

WHY IT WORKS

When the rulers are tapped near the tube, the sound seems to come from the left. When you point the tube to the wall, you hear the sound in your left ear and a separate sound in your right ear. This is because sound travels slowly, hits the wall and bounces back down the tube. So your brain detects a separate sound.

The speed at which sound travels depends upon the material it travels through. Sound travels 15 times faster through steel than it does through air.

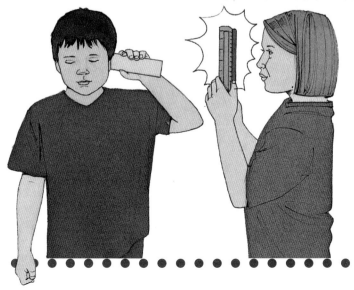

15

Hearing sound

The vibrations that form a sound wave can be detected by the eardrum in your ear. The eardrum vibrates and our brain interprets this vibration as sound. Young people can hear a wide range of different sound waves, but as people get older the range they can hear gets smaller. Many animals can detect sound waves that humans can't hear.

Make a model ear to see how your ear works

METHOD NOTES
Take care when cutting the foil tray – it can be sharp.

Materials
- modelling clay
- bendy drinking straw
- table tennis ball
- foil tray
- cling film
- glue
- sticky tape
- bowl of water
- scissors

1. Cut out a hole from the bottom of the foil tray (Figure 1).

Figure 1

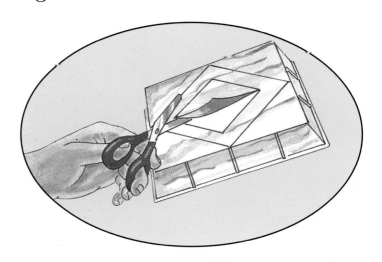

Figure 2

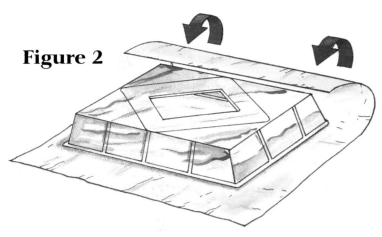

2. Stretch the cling film over the top of the tray (Figure 2) and tape it in place.

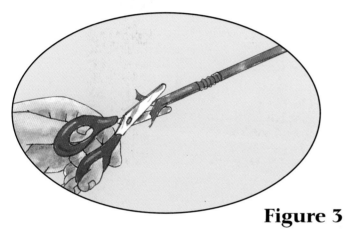

Figure 3

3. Cut four slits about 1 cm long in each end of the bendy straw (Figure 3).

4. Glue the end nearest to the bend of the straw onto the table tennis ball (Figure 4).

5. Tape the other end of the straw to the middle of the cling film opposite the hole in the tray (Figure 5).

Figure 4

6. Place the foil tray on its side and push it firmly into the modelling clay (Figure 5).

7. Position a bowl of water on the table so that the table tennis ball rests on the surface of the water (Figure 5).

8. Speak into the base of the foil tray and watch what happens to the water.

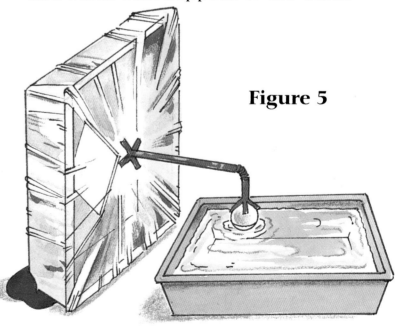

Figure 5

WHY IT WORKS

Sound waves from your voice make the cling film vibrate. This vibrates the straw and the ball, causing ripples in the water. When your eardrum vibrates, it causes vibrations in a fluid in your ear, which your brain interprets as sound.

Hearing sound

MAKE A STETHOSCOPE

Push the end of a small funnel onto the end of a piece of rubber tube. Hold the wide part of the funnel of your stethoscope up against the left side of someone's chest.

Put your ear to the tube and listen to their heartbeat. Then try and listen to their heartbeat just using the tube, without the funnel. Can you hear it now? You probably won't hear the heartbeat without the funnel. The funnel collects lots of the sound waves and directs them down the tube into your ear. This makes the sound seem louder.

MAKE A SOUND DISH

Connect a funnel to a rubber tube. Wedge a wok or a bowl in modelling clay on its side, on a table. Let it face a wind-up clock about 6 metres away. Hold the tube to your ear and point the funnel towards the wok. The wok and funnel collect the sound waves so you can hear the ticking of the clock much more clearly.

18

That's tiny!
Did you know that the stapes (one of the three bones in the ear) is the smallest bone in the human body? It is about 3 mm long and weighs about 3 mg.

Figure 1

MAKE A TELEPHONE

Use a pencil and modelling clay to make a hole in the bottom of 2 paper cups (Figure 1). Push one end of a long piece of string through the bottom of one cup. Attach a paper clip to the end of the string in the cup. Do the same with the other end of the string and the other cup. Move the cups apart so the string is taut. Speak into one cup while a friend listens to the other one (Figure 2).

Figure 2

WHY IT WORKS

When you talk into the cup, the air in the cup vibrates. This causes the sides of the cup, the string and the second cup to vibrate. The vibrations are detected by your ear as sound.

Sound spreads out in all directions. The further you are from a sound, the quieter it seems. Loudness is measured in decibels (dB). Whispering is about 30 dB and thunder is about 100 dB.

Sound in nature

Animals use sound as a warning signal, a mating call and to show that they are hungry. Although they sound the same to humans, the sounds that baby animals make are very individual so that their parents can find them if they are lost. It's not just animals that make sound. If you have ever heard a thunderstorm you will know that sounds in nature can be extremely loud.

Make the sound of a seagull

METHOD NOTES
Make sure you push the two yoghurt pots as close together as you can.

Materials

- 2 yoghurt pots
- modelling clay
- a sweet tube
- a pencil
- glue

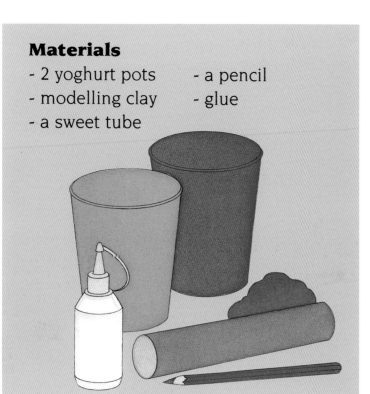

1. Put a piece of modelling clay onto a hard surface. Place a yoghurt pot on top of the modelling clay. Pierce a 0.5 cm hole in the bottom of the yoghurt pot using a sharp pencil (Figure 1). Do the same with the other yoghurt pot.

Figure 1

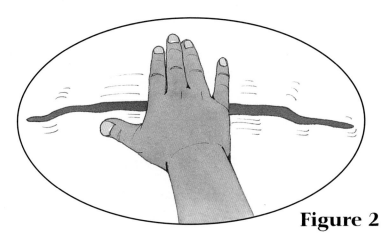

Figure 2

2. Roll out a length of modelling clay into a sausage shape (Figure 2).

3. Wrap it around the rim of one of the yoghurt pots.

4. Place the other yoghurt pot into the first one and press down. Make sure that the rim of the second pot presses into the modelling clay on the first pot (Figure 3).

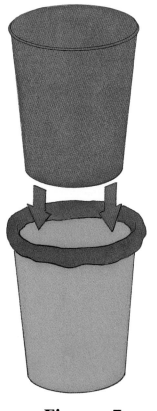

Figure 3

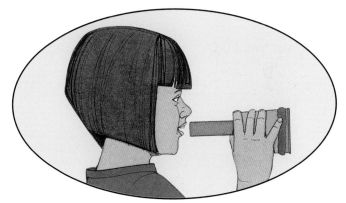

Figure 4

5. Take off the lid and remove the bottom of the sweet tube.

6. Glue the tube onto the base of the yoghurt pot so that it covers the hole (Figure 4).

7. Blow through the tube (Figure 5).

Figure 5

WHY IT WORKS

As you blow down the tube, air is channelled towards the hole in the pot. The vibrating air is squeezed between the two pots. This makes the inside pot vibrate and create the seagull sound. Seagulls use sound to warn predators from their young and to attract a mate.

Sound in nature

Many animals have very large ears to collect sound. This gives them early warning of any approaching danger.

ANIMAL SOUNDS

Animals make many different sounds. These sounds can come from various parts of their body. Some make a noise by using their vocal cords, and others use their tail, wings, feet or head.

a

b

c

d

e

f

g

What parts of their body do these animals use to create sound? Match the animals above with the body parts below.

Body parts		
beak	head	tongue
cheeks	mouth	vocal cords
feet	tails	wings

answers:
a. wings b. vocal cords/mouth c. vocal cords/wings/beak d. vocal cords/throat/cheeks e. feet/vocal cords f. tail/tongue g. head

Whales that sing
Sound travels quickly through water. Whales communicate using low-pitched sounds that other whales hear hundreds of kilometres away.

THE AMAZING OCEAN IN A SHELL
Find out what you can hear in a sea shell

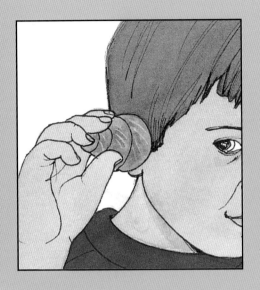

Next time you are at the beach, find a large, enclosed seashell – the bigger the better. Stand on the beach and hold it up to your ear and listen.

WHY IT WORKS

You hear the sound of the sea inside the shell. The shell captures and amplifies the background sounds that are all around you. When you are at the beach it amplifies the sound of the sea. This is what you hear when you listen to the shell.

LISTEN UNDERWATER

Take two wide-mouthed glasses and fill one to the top with water. Put your ear inside the empty one. Tap the glass with a knife. Now submerge your ear in the water in the second glass, and tap this glass with a knife. How is the sound different?

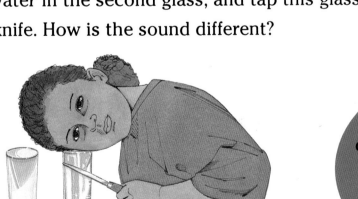

Animal sounds usually have a certain function. Animals make sounds when protecting their territory, attracting a mate and calling their young.

Musical sound

Music is a collection of different sound waves. Musical sounds are called notes and are made in the same way all sounds are – by vibration. When you play the piano each key moves a hammer, which hits a string and makes it vibrate. A violin bow makes the strings vibrate. When you play a wind instrument, your lips or a special reed vibrate to create the musical sound.

Make instruments to see how sound can be amplified

METHOD NOTES
Make sure you hold the cup very lightly near the top.

Materials
- 2 pieces of string
- a paper cup

- 2 paper clips
- water
- a nail
- a ruler
- a pencil
- modelling clay

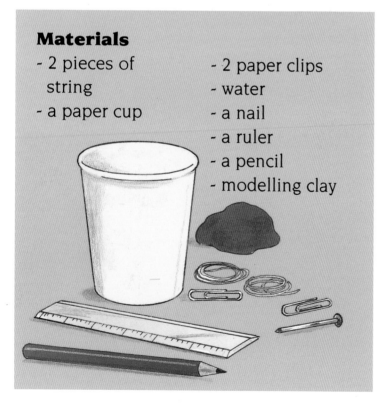

1. Tie a paper clip to the end of one piece of string (Figure 1). Make sure it is tied tightly and won't come undone.
2. Hold the piece of string by the paperclip and dip the fingers of your other hand in some water.

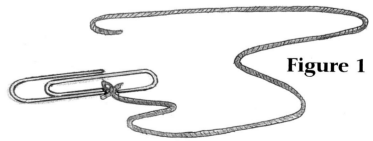

Figure 1

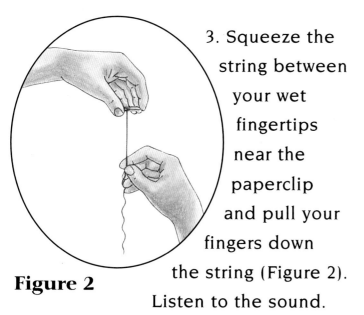

Figure 2

3. Squeeze the string between your wet fingertips near the paperclip and pull your fingers down the string (Figure 2). Listen to the sound.

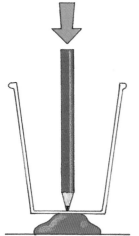

Figure 3

4. Carefully pierce a hole in the bottom of the cup (Figure 3).
5. Tie a paperclip to the end of the other piece of string.

6. Thread the end of the string without the paper clip through the hole in the cup (Figure 4).

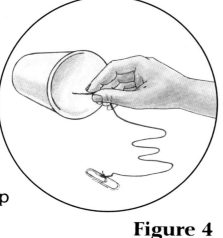

Figure 4

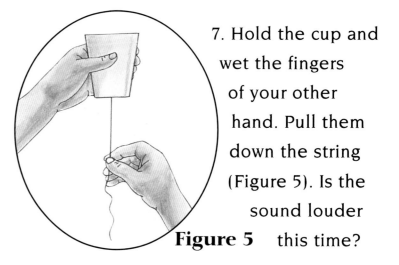

7. Hold the cup and wet the fingers of your other hand. Pull them down the string (Figure 5). Is the sound louder this time?

Figure 5

8. Tie a nail to the end of the string attached to the cup. Hit the nail with a ruler (Figure 6). Listen to the sound.

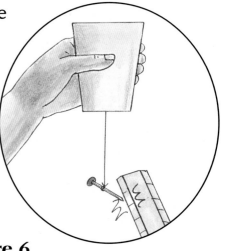

Figure 6

WHY IT WORKS

When you pull your fingers down the string, the string vibrates. Vibrations travel to the cup. The cup and the air in it vibrate and amplify the sound. Without the cup, the sound is quieter. The same principle applies with the nail. Vibrations from hitting the nail travel up the string to the cup where the sound is amplified.

Create musical sound

MUSICAL BOTTLES

Carefully fill three bottles with different levels of water. Place the bottles in a line. Make sure they are spaced slightly apart.

Blow horizontally across the top of each bottle (Figure 1) and listen to the different sounds.

Figure 1

This time, the fuller the bottle, the higher the note. This is the opposite way round to the water xylophone on page 27.

WHY IT WORKS

The shorter the column of air inside a bottle, the faster the air vibrates. Blowing across a bottle with more water in it makes a higher note.

A silent piano?
Did you know that if you played a musical instrument on the moon, you wouldn't be able to hear it? Sound waves cannot travel in space as there is no air.

MAKE A REED PIPE

Flatten the end of a straw using a butter knife (Figure 1). Use a skewer to carefully punch holes in one side of the straw.

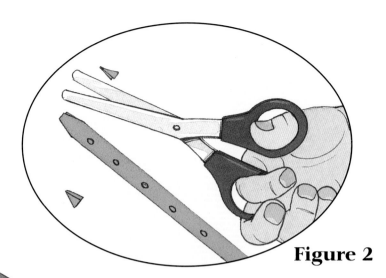

Figure 2

Figure 1

Cut off each corner of the flattened end of the straw (Figure 2). Place the flattened end in your mouth and blow. Cover and uncover the holes with your fingers to make different sounds.

WHY IT WORKS

When you blow into the straw, the flattened tip vibrates very quickly. This causes the column of air in the straw to vibrate, creating a sound. By covering the holes, the length of the column of air increases and makes a lower sound.

MAKE A RECORDER

Make holes in a cardboard tube. Fix wax paper over one end of the tube using an elastic band. Put the other end to your mouth and hum into it. Change the pitch by covering the holes. The sound makes the paper vibrate and the tube amplifies the sound of your voice.

Sounds can be loud or soft. When an instrument makes a loud sound, it is making a big vibration. The size of each vibration is called its amplitude. The louder a sound, the bigger the amplitude.

Noise

An aeroplane taking off, a crowd cheering at a football game or machinery working are all noisy sounds. As we have learnt, the loudness of a sound is measured in decibels (dB). Noises louder than 130 dB are painful to our ears. A rocket launch can be as loud as 190 dB. Next time you are in the playground, stop for a minute and listen to just how noisy human beings can be too!

Make a paper banger to hear a loud noise

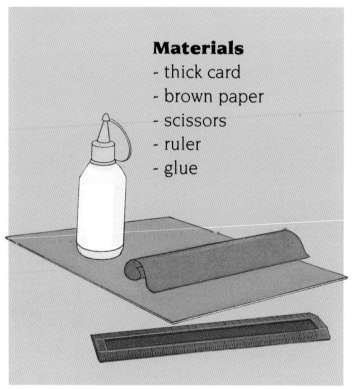

Materials
- thick card
- brown paper
- scissors
- ruler
- glue

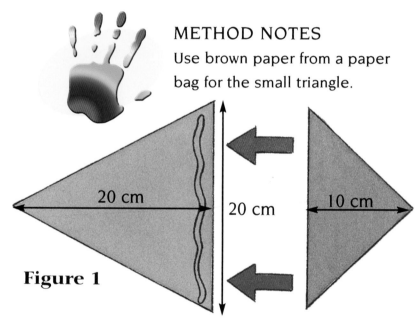

METHOD NOTES
Use brown paper from a paper bag for the small triangle.

20 cm

20 cm

10 cm

Figure 1

1. Cut out a triangle shape from the thick card, 20 cm width by 20 cm in length (Figure 1).
2. Cut out another triangle shape from the brown paper, 10 cm width by 20 cm in length (Figure 1).

Figure 2

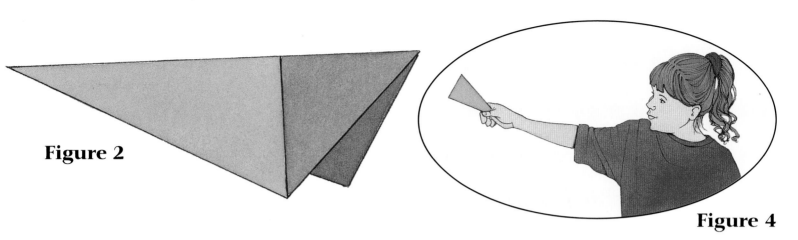

3. Carefully glue the two shapes together (Figure 1).

4. Fold the shape in half along the middle (Figure 2).

7. Pull your arm down sharply so that the brown triangle snaps out (Figure 5).

Figure 4

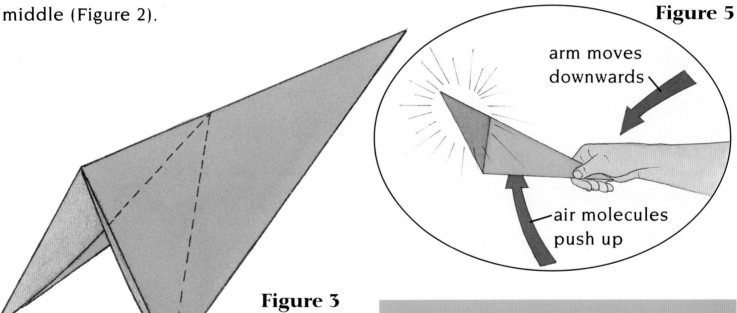

Figure 5

arm moves downwards

air molecules push up

Figure 3

5. Tuck the brown paper triangle under the cardboard triangle (Figure 3).

6. Hold the banger away from your body with your arm straight and pointing slightly upwards (Figure 4).

WHY IT WORKS

As you pull downwards, air rushes underneath the cardboard triangle. The air pushes the brown paper out with a bang. The noise is made by the paper striking the air and causing it to vibrate in short, sharp shock waves.

Noise

EXPERIMENT WITH NOISE

Blow up a balloon but don't tie it. Stretch the neck of the balloon and slowly let some air out (Figure 1). Listen to the noise it makes. Blow up the balloon again and tie it. Pop the balloon with a pin (Figure 2).

Figure 2

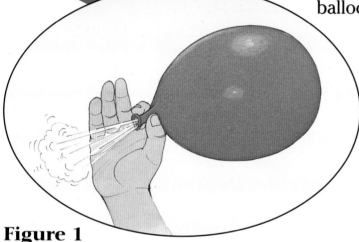

Figure 1

How is the noise different each time? When you stretch the neck of the balloon and release the air, the balloon neck vibrates very quickly and makes a high-pitched squeak.

When you pop the balloon, all the air is suddenly released. The sudden release of air causes shock waves. Shock waves are what we hear as bangs and explosions.

The loudest noise ever!
Did you know that the loudest noise ever recorded was a volcanic eruption in 1883 in Krakatoa? The explosion could be heard 5,000 km away.

MAKE A SIREN

Use a skewer to carefully make a hole in the bottom of an empty can.

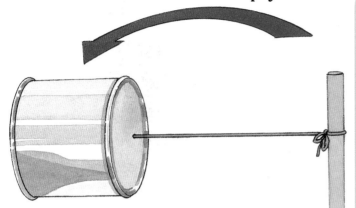

Thread a long piece of thick string through the hole – be careful of sharp edges. Tie a knot at the end inside the can so the string can't slip through the hole. Coat the string in rosin. Tie the string loosely round some dowelling. Carefully whirl the can around your head. What sound does it make?

WHY IT WORKS

Because the string is coated in rosin, it continuously sticks to and unsticks from the dowelling as it spins. This friction makes the string vibrate. The vibration travels to the can where it is amplified. This vibration causes a siren sound.

THE AMAZING WAILER
Make an elastic band wail

Bend a wire into a horseshoe shape. Stretch an elastic band across the ends. Make sure it is taut. Firmly tie the end of a metre of string to the middle of the horseshoe. Hold the other end and carefully whirl it round your head.

WHY IT WORKS

As the wailer spins, the air makes the elastic band vibrate and make a wailing noise. The faster you whirl it, the faster it vibrates and the higher it wails.

Some places need to be insulated against noise. Recording studios have sound-proofing in their walls so that background noise doesn't spoil the recording.

Echoes & acoustics

An echo is the sound produced when sound waves are reflected off an object, like when you shout in a big tunnel. You can't hear an echo in a small room because the sound bounces back from the walls too quickly for you to hear. To hear an echo you must be in a large, empty place, at a distance from a hard wall. The way sound travels in a room is called acoustics.

Make an echo chamber to hear acoustics at work

METHOD NOTES
Be careful piercing the holes in the tube.

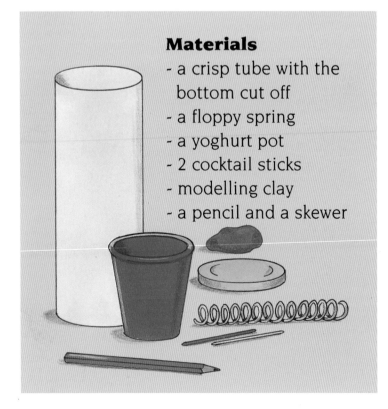

Materials
- a crisp tube with the bottom cut off
- a floppy spring
- a yoghurt pot
- 2 cocktail sticks
- modelling clay
- a pencil and a skewer

1. Stretch the floppy spring so that it doubles in length. Make a mark on the tube at the height of the stretched spring (Figure 1).

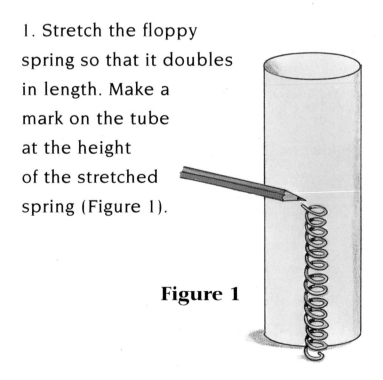

Figure 1

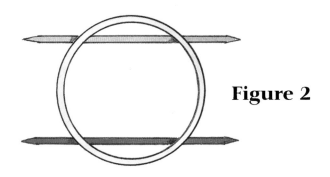

Figure 2

5. Make a hole in the lid of the tube (Figure 4).
6. Put the yoghurt pot and the spring inside the tube and rest the pot on the cocktail sticks (Figure 5).

2. At the mark on the tube, use a skewer to make four holes so that you can push two cocktail sticks through the tube (Figure 2).
3. Make a hole in the bottom of the yoghurt pot with the skewer.
4. Push one end of the spring through the hole (Figure 3).

Figure 3

Figure 4

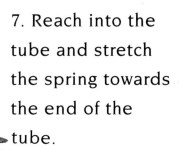

7. Reach into the tube and stretch the spring towards the end of the tube.

8. Twist the end of the spring through the hole in the lid and put the lid on the tube (Figure 5).
9. Speak into the open end of the tube to hear your voice echo.

Figure 5

WHY IT WORKS

When you speak into the tube, the vibrations of your voice cause the pot and the spring to vibrate. Vibrations are reflected from the spring to the sides of the tube and back. The pot amplifies the echoes, making it sound like you are speaking in a long tunnel.

Echoes & acoustics

Echoes are only produced when sound waves bounce off hard objects. When sound hits a soft object, the object absorbs the sound and muffles it.

MAKE A RIPPLE TANK

Bend a thin strip of cardboard, metal or plastic into a curved shape (Figure 1). Place the strip at the far end of a baking tray.

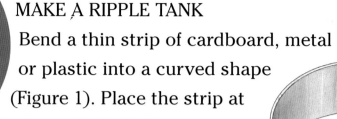

Figure 1

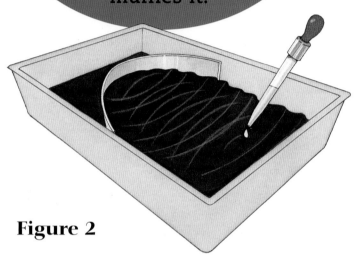

Figure 2

Fill the tray with water and add some black ink. Stir it. Using an eyedropper drip some drops of water into the middle of the tray (Figure 2). Watch what happens to the ripples of the water.

WHY IT WORKS

As the ripples hit the curved metal strip they are reflected back in lines. The drop of water dropped into the tray represents a sound being made. Sound waves spread out in all directions until they hit a hard surface. Then they are reflected back as an echo.

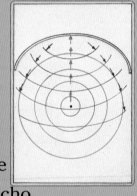

Seeing with sound

Bats make high-pitched sounds while flying. These sounds bounce off objects and tell the bat the location and distance of these objects. They can catch prey, even in darkness!

36

THE AMAZING ROBOT VOICE
See how echoes change the sound of your voice

Sit facing an electric fan. Be careful not to get too close. Switch the fan on and say something out loud. Listen to the sound of your voice.

WHY IT WORKS

As you speak, sound waves spread out towards the fan. They bounce off the fan blades as the blades turn. Some of the sound waves travel through the gaps between the blades and are not reflected back. So only some of your voice is reflected and your voice sounds like that of a robot's.

HEARING ECHOES

Stand in a long hall or tunnel. Shout loudly. Listen for the echo. Now shout again but this time push your ears forwards. The echo sounds louder the second time because your hands and ears capture more of the reflected sound.

Ships use sonar to see. A picture of the ocean bed is formed by timing how long it takes a high-pitched sound to travel to and bounce back from the ocean floor.

Resonance

Everything has a natural speed at which it vibrates. This is called its natural frequency. If you open a piano and sing a note into it, the appropriate string picks up the vibrations of your voice. This causes the string to vibrate at its natural frequency so that you hear a note coming from the piano. When the vibrations of one thing make something else vibrate, it is called resonance.

See resonance in action

METHOD NOTES

It doesn't matter what objects you use for this experiment, as long as one of them is much heavier than the rest.

Materials
- string and scissors
- two chairs
- four spoons
- an empty detergent bottle
- a funnel

1. Put the funnel in the top of the detergent bottle and carefully fill it with water (Figure 1). Make sure it is filled almost to the top and then put the lid on tightly.

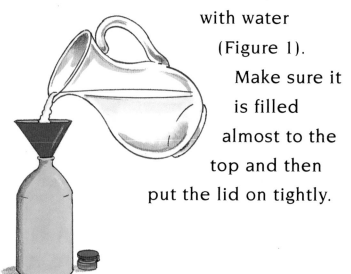

Figure 1

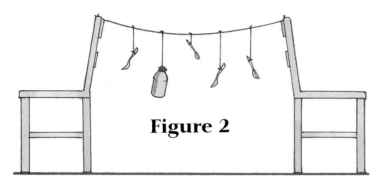

Figure 2

2. Cut five pieces of string. Two of the pieces must be exactly the same length, the others can be any length.

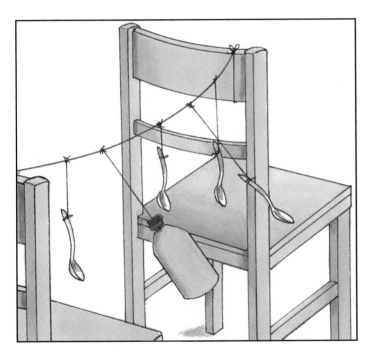

Figure 3

3. Take the two identical lengths of string and tie one to the bottle and one to a spoon.

4. Then tie the other three pieces of string to the other objects.

5. Cut a long piece of string and tie it between the two chairs so that it is taut.

6. Tie the objects to the long string (Figure 2).

7. Swing the bottle and watch what happens to the other objects (Figure 3).

WHY IT WORKS

When you swing the bottle, both the string it is tied to and the long piece of string vibrate. The identical length of string also starts to vibrate and swing. The other lengths don't move. The identical strings have the same natural frequency. The vibration of one sound makes an object with the same natural frequency vibrate and make a sound.

Collapsing bridges

Did you know that bridges can collapse because of vibration? The vibration caused by lots of people marching in step across a bridge can make it sway and break apart.

Resonance & vibration

Resonance can make sounds louder. A guitar string vibrates when it is plucked. The air in the guitar resonates to make the note louder.

VIBRATING SOUNDS

A plane going overhead causes vibrations at lots of different frequencies. These sounds bounce off the ground as echoes, and cancel out the sounds that are coming directly from the plane to you. The higher sounds are cancelled out before the lower ones. If you bend down, you can hear all the frequencies, and planes' sounds have a higher pitch. As you stand up, the higher sounds are cancelled out. The higher you are the lower the pitch of the sounds of the plane.

WHISTLING TUBE

Fill a jar partway with water. Lower a cardboard tube into the water by a couple of centimetres. Whistle across the top of the tube and at the same time raise and lower the tube. Try the tube at lots of different heights in the water.

WHY IT WORKS

At a certain point, your whistle will become louder. This is when the column of air inside the tube is resonating at the same frequency as your whistle.

THE AMAZING SINGING GLASS
See how to make a glass sing

Dip your finger into water. Carefully slide your finger around the lip of a crystal glass until the glass begins to 'sing'. Only do this for a short time.

WHY IT WORKS

When you slide your finger around the edge of the glass, the glass vibrates at its natural frequency. The air in the glass begins to vibrate at the same frequency, amplifying the sound of the glass 'singing'.

MAKE A SQUEALING ROD

Put some rosin on the thumb and index finger of one of your hands. Hold a metre-long aluminium rod in the middle with the thumb and one finger of your other hand. Stroke the rod lengthwise from the centre to the end using your rosin-coated thumb and finger (Figure 1). The rod will begin to vibrate and squeal. If you dip the end in water while the rod is still squealing, you will see ripples in the water (Figure 2).

Figure 1

Resonance is very powerful. If you tap a glass it will vibrate at its natural frequency. If you make a very loud sound at exactly the natural frequency of the glass, you could shatter the glass.

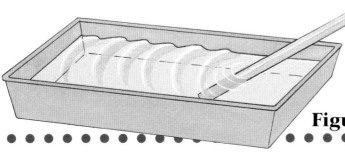

Figure 2

Wonderful sound

Sound can be used to express anger, fear and danger as well as joy, happiness and celebration. Animals often need sound to communicate with each other. Human beings need sound to be able to talk, sing, shout and scream. Walk down the street and you will hear sound coming from almost everything – the wind blowing, your footsteps and birds singing.

Make a rainstick to recreate the sound of rain

METHOD NOTES
If you don't have toothpicks for this experiment you can use cocktail sticks.

Materials
- 2 or 3 paper towel tubes
- toothpicks
- sticky tape
- a plastic bag
- elastic bands
- dried lentils
- paints
- lollipop sticks
- a drawing pin

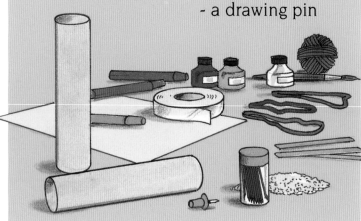

1. Tape the ends of the tubes together to make one long tube (Figure 1).
2. Cut a circle from a plastic bag that is big enough to cover the end of the tube.

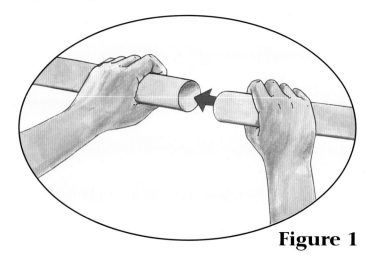

Figure 1

42

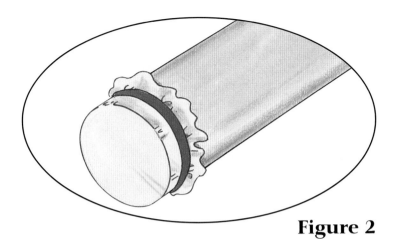

Figure 2

3. Put the circle of plastic over one end of the long tube. Secure it with an elastic band (Figure 2).

4. Tape three lollipop sticks over the joint where the tubes meet (Figure 3).

Figure 3

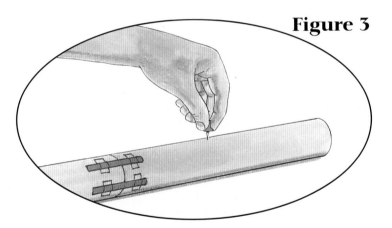

5. Decorate your tube with the paints.

6. Using a drawing pin, push holes into the side of the tube (Figure 3) in a line that spirals around the tube from top to bottom.

7. Count how many holes you have made. Take this many toothpicks and blunt one end of each of them by pushing it onto a hard surface.

8. Push the pointed end of each toothpick through a hole until it touches the other side.

Figure 4

9. Do this all the way along the tube. The more toothpicks the better.

10. Fill the tube half full of lentils (Figure 4). Cover the open end in the same way as you did in steps 2 and 3.

11. Turn your finished rainstick (Figure 5) upside down and listen.

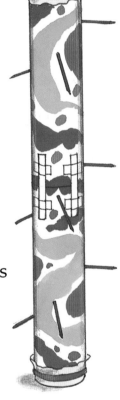

Figure 5

WHY IT WORKS

When you turn the tube upside down, the lentils bounce off the toothpicks and hit the walls and each other. This creates a sound like rain falling.

Wonderful sound

Human languages use many different sounds, including strange clicks and pops. Sounds like 'k' and 'p' and 't' are sounds we make without using our voices.

LEARN TO WHISTLE

Make your upper and lower lips cover your teeth and tuck them into your mouth. Take your right and left index fingers (Figure 1) and place them roughly halfway between the corners and centre of your lips. Insert them up to the first knuckle.

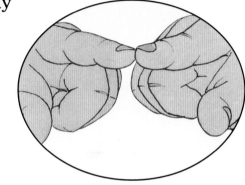

Figure 1

Figure 2

Pull your bottom lip taut with your fingers (Figure 2). Make sure the tip of your tongue is almost touching the bottom of your mouth. Blow hard and keep adjusting your fingers and tongue to get a really loud whistle.

Fat pig!
Ultrasonic echoes are used by farmers to measure how much fat animals have. Doctors use ultrasonic echoes to create pictures of babies in the womb.

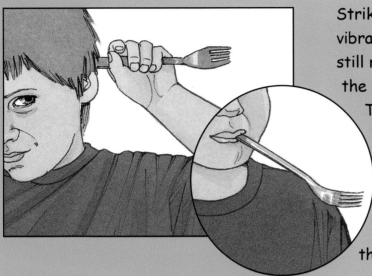

Strike a fork against a table. Listen to it vibrate and make a ringing sound. While it is still ringing, press the handle of the fork on the bone behind your ear. Does it sound loud? Then bite the handle of the fork while it is still ringing. Does this sound louder still?

WHY IT WORKS

The vibrations make the bones in your ear or mouth vibrate. Sound travels through bone and teeth better than through air. So it sounds louder this way.

Figure 1

PLAY THE COMB

Fold a piece of wax paper in half. Wrap the paper round a comb (Figure 1). Hold the comb to your lips (Figure 2) and hum onto it. Listen to the sound as the paper vibrates.

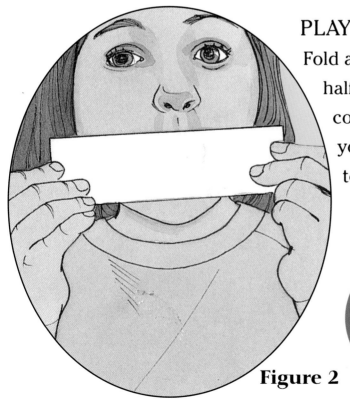

Figure 2

Sound is all around you. Try covering your ears and see how different the world would be without sound!

Glossary

Acoustics

Sound waves are reflected off walls when sounds are made in a room. The way that sound travels in a room is called acoustics.

Amplify

When a sound is amplified it is made louder. Objects that collect sound waves, such as a funnel or a dish, can amplify sounds.

Amplitude

The loudness of sound is called its amplitude. A loud sound has a big amplitude and a quiet sound has a small amplitude.

Decibels

The loudness of sound is measured in decibels. The loudness of conversation is about 60 decibels (dB).

Doppler effect

When a sound source travels toward you, the sound raises in pitch; when the sound source travels away from you, the sound lowers in pitch. This is known as the Doppler effect.

Eardrum

A thin piece of skin inside your ear. Sound waves make it vibrate and your brain detects this movement as sound.

Echoes

Echoes are sounds that have bounced off a hard surface and are heard after the first sound has been made.

Frequency

The frequency is the number of sound vibrations that happen in a second. The higher the frequency, the higher the pitch of the note. Everything has a natural frequency at which it vibrates.

Pitch

Pitch describes how high or low a note is. A high note has a high pitch and a low note has a low pitch. The higher the pitch, the faster the sound waves are vibrating.

Resonance

When the vibrations of one thing make something else vibrate, this is called resonance. Resonance can make sounds louder.

Sonar

The way in which ships and some animals bounce sound off objects to get a picture of their surroundings.

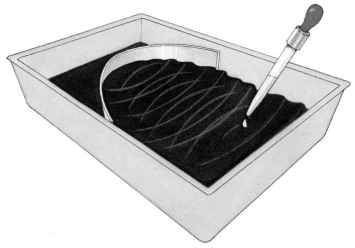

Sound waves

A regular pattern of vibrations that can move through air or other materials. Sound waves spread out in all directions from their source in a similar way to ripples spreading out in water.

Stethoscope

An instrument used by doctors to listen to the sounds in your body that you can't usually hear, such as your heartbeat.

Ultrasonic sound

Sound waves that have a very high pitch. The sound is so high that humans cannot hear it.

Vibration

When something moves backwards and forwards very quickly it is said to be vibrating.

Index

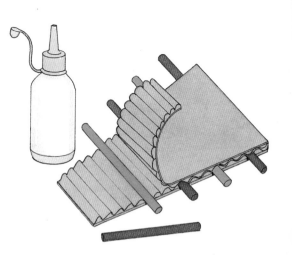